It's My
STATE!

ILLINOIS
The Prairie State

John Micklos Jr., Claire Price-Groff,
Elizabeth Kaplan, and Gerry Boehme

Cavendish
Square

New York

Published in 2020 by Cavendish Square Publishing, LLC
243 5th Avenue, Suite 136, New York, NY 10016

Copyright © 2020 by Cavendish Square Publishing, LLC

Fourth Edition

Library of Congress Cataloging-in-Publication Data

Names: Micklos, John, author. | Price-Groff, Claire, author. | Kaplan, Elizabeth, author. | Boehme, Gerry, author.
Title: Illinois / John Micklos Jr., Claire Price-Groff, Elizabeth Kaplan, and Gerry Boehme.
Description: Fourth edition. | New York: Cavendish Square, 2020 |
Series: It's my state! | Includes bibliographical references and index.
Identifiers: LCCN 2018048000 (print) | LCCN 2018049810 (ebook) |
ISBN 9781502642172 (ebook) | ISBN 9781502642165 (library bound) | ISBN 9781502644534 (pbk.)
Subjects: LCSH: Illinois--Juvenile literature.
Classification: LCC F541.3 (ebook) | LCC F541.3 .P75 2019 (print) | DDC 977.3--dc23
LC record available at https://lccn.loc.gov/2018048000

Editorial Director: David McNamara
Editor: Caitlyn Miller
Copy Editor: Nathan Heidelberger
Associate Art Director: Alan Sliwinski
Designer: Jessica Nevins
Production Coordinator: Karol Szymczuk
Photo Research: J8 Media

It's My STATE!

Table of Contents

INTRODUCTION
SNAPSHOT ILLINOIS 4

ONE
GEOGRAPHY 9

TWO
THE HISTORY OF ILLINOIS 23

THREE
WHO LIVES IN ILLINOIS? 45

FOUR
AT WORK IN ILLINOIS 59

FIVE
GOVERNMENT 69

Glossary 75 • Illinois State Map and Map
Skills 77 • More Information 78 • Index 79

SNAPSHOT
ILLINOIS

The Prairie State

Statehood

December 3, 1818

Population

12,802,023
(2017 census estimate)

Capital

Springfield

State Seal

The state seal of Illinois features an eagle carrying a banner in its beak and a shield in its talons. The banner bears the state's motto: "State sovereignty, national union." This motto celebrates the state's rights and its role in the United States as a whole. At the bottom is the date Illinois adopted its constitution: August 26, 1818. In the background, the sun rises over water. The words "Seal of the State of Illinois" are at the top of the seal. The present seal was adopted in 1868.

State Flag

The state flag features the state seal on a white background. The first state flag was adopted in 1915. Lucy Derwent's design was selected from among thirty-five entries in a contest sponsored by the Daughters of the American Revolution. In 1970, the word "Illinois" was added to the bottom of the flag.

HISTORICAL EVENTS TIMELINE

1673
Louis Jolliet and Jacques Marquette explore what is now Illinois.

1818
Illinois becomes a state.

1871
The Great Chicago Fire destroys most of Chicago.

State Song

The state song, "Illinois," touches on both the state's nickname of "Prairie State" and its status as a commercial hub. One of the few state songs to talk about people, it refers to Abraham Lincoln, Ulysses S. Grant, and John Logan, a Civil War general and politician. Charles H. Chamberlain wrote the words for "Illinois" in the 1890s, and Archibald Johnston composed the music. "Illinois" became the state song in 1925. In 1966, Win Stracke wrote two additional verses for the song, making six in all.

State Flower

In 1907, schoolchildren across the state of Illinois selected the violet as the state flower. The Illinois General Assembly made it official a year later. Eight varieties of the bluish-purple flower grow in the state. They can be found on the prairies, as well as in woods and wetlands. New Jersey, Rhode Island, and Wisconsin also have the violet as the state flower.

State Tree

For many years, the state tree of Illinois was the native oak. In 1973, a special poll of nine hundred thousand schoolchildren voted the white oak as the state tree. Found throughout the eastern and central United States, the white oak typically grows to a height of between 60 and 100 feet (18 and 30 meters). Connecticut and Maryland also have the white oak as their state tree.

1885

The world's first skyscraper, the Home Insurance Building, opens in Illinois.

1919

Illinois is one of the first states to ratify the Nineteenth Amendment, which allows women to vote.

1942

The first controlled **nuclear** fission chain reaction takes place at the University of Chicago.

State Animal
White-Tailed Deer

State Bird
Cardinal

1998

The Chicago Bulls, led by Michael Jordan, win their sixth NBA title of the decade.

2003

Emil Jones becomes the first African American president of the Illinois state senate.

2005

The Abraham Lincoln Presidential Library and Museum opens in Springfield.

State Insect
Monarch
Butterfly

State Fossil
Tully Monster

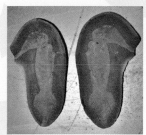

State Snack
Popcorn

CURRENT EVENTS TIMELINE

2008
Former Illinois senator
Barack Obama is elected
US President and serves
two terms.

2016
The Chicago Cubs win
the World Series for the
first time in more than
a century.

2018
Illinois celebrates
two hundred years of
statehood with special
events throughout
the state.

Chicago, the largest city in Illinois, is home to 2.7 million people.

1 Geography

The Prairie State features far more than wheat fields and farms. The state has the nation's third-largest city, Chicago, as well as dozens of midsize and small towns. Water plays a key role in shaping the state's geography. The Mississippi, Ohio, and Wabash Rivers all flow through Illinois or form one of its borders. Meanwhile, Chicago sits on the shore of Lake Michigan, one of the nation's five Great Lakes. From fields and forests to lakes and rivers, Illinois offers something for everyone.

Regions of Illinois

There are different types of terrain in the northwestern section of the state. That is where you will find Illinois's highest points and deepest valleys. Jagged limestone cliffs and rocky outcrops break up hilly prairies. The northwestern portion of the state also has wetlands and forests.

Northeast Illinois has rich plains dotted with small lakes and marshes. Much of the farmland that once covered the region has given way to cities. Chicago is located in the eastern section of those plains. The southern end of Lake Michigan serves as the northeastern border of the state.

FAST FACT

The Mississippi River forms the western border of Illinois. At 2,340 miles (3,766 kilometers), it's the second-longest river in North America. By some measures, it's 100 miles (161 km) shorter than the Missouri River. For centuries, the Mississippi River has been a key waterway for the United States.

Illinois borders Wisconsin, Indiana, Kentucky, Missouri, and Iowa.

Rolling wheat fields cover much of central and southern Illinois.

The central portion of Illinois boasts some of the most fertile soil in the United States. Flat land covers much of the area, perfect for farming. However, gently rolling hills also add variety to the landscape. The hills were created millions of years ago when glaciers—large bodies of ice—moved across the earth, bringing rich soil to the region. The glaciers also carved high ridges, deep canyons, and caves across south central Illinois. The soil in the south central part of the state, however, is mostly clay and is not good for farming.

The western portion of Illinois, between the Illinois and Mississippi Rivers, has many hills, valleys, small lakes, and streams. This west central area of the state is perfect for people who love fishing, boating, and mountain biking. Many miles of trails have been developed to help people enjoy that sport.

To the south are the Illinois Ozarks, a hilly region with impressive sandstone cliffs and deep canyons. Unlike the level central landscape, glaciers did not create this rugged terrain. The Shawnee National Forest stretches across the region, covering more than 280,000 acres (113,300 hectares). The only national forest in Illinois, it is a popular place for hiking, camping, canoeing, and horseback riding. Within the Shawnee National Forest is the Garden of the Gods wilderness area. Large rock formations, sculpted by the wind into interesting shapes, give this part of the forest its name. Hikers in the Garden of the Gods can see rocks in unusual shapes, including a camel, a mushroom, a smokestack, and a table.

Two large rivers, the Ohio and the Mississippi, bound the southern part of the state. This region is sometimes called Egypt, or Little Egypt. One explanation for these nicknames is that the majestic rivers made early European American settlers think of the Nile River in Egypt. The southernmost city in Illinois is Cairo (in Illinois pronounced "CARE-oh"), which is named after that famous Egyptian city.

The Garden of the Gods wilderness area offers incredible scenery.

Rivers and Lakes

Waterways abound in Illinois. The Mississippi River cuts western Illinois into a series of notches as it flows south. Lake Michigan, one of the five Great Lakes, sits at the state's northeast corner. The Wabash River separates southeastern Illinois from Indiana. The Ohio River forms the border between southern Illinois and Kentucky. The Illinois River drains a large area across the central portion of the state. Almost all the rivers in Illinois, large or small, eventually flow into the Mississippi. Many of these rivers are great for fishing, which is popular throughout Illinois.

The Cairo Ohio River Bridge in southern Illinois sits near the spot where the Ohio and Mississippi Rivers meet.

Illinois's most important port city is Chicago on Lake Michigan. By area, Lake Michigan is the fourth-largest freshwater lake in the world. A person standing on its shore cannot see across it to the opposite side. Illinois has several other large lakes, including Carlyle Lake and Rend Lake. Many large lakes in Illinois were created when a dam was built across a river.

Illinois's Biggest Cities

(Population numbers are from the US Census Bureau's 2017 projections for incorporated cities.)

Aurora

Naperville

1. Chicago: population 2,716,450

The third-largest city in the United States, Chicago sits on the shore of Lake Michigan. While the city itself has more than 2.7 million people, the surrounding area ("**Chicagoland**") contains nearly 10 million people in three states: Illinois, Wisconsin, and Indiana.

2. Aurora: population 200,965

Located on the western edge of Greater Chicago, Aurora has grown impressively over the past half century. It is known as the "City of Lights." Aurora got this nickname because it installed fully electric street lights in 1881, making it one of the first US cities to do so.

3. Joliet: population 148,462

Once an industrial city, Joliet entered a period of economic decline in the late 1970s and 1980s. Joliet's economy rebounded in the 1990s, and now millions of people visit its riverboat casinos, drag racing, and NASCAR tracks.

4. Naperville: population 147,682

Considered to be a western suburb of Chicago, Naperville was once known for farming and manufacturing but has evolved into an affluent city. In 2012, Naperville was listed on *Money* magazine's Top 100 Best Places to Live.

5. Rockford: population 147,051

Located halfway between Chicago and Galena, the community was also briefly known as "Midway." Thousands of Swedish **immigrants** settled in Rockford between 1835 and the early 1900s, and their history is still celebrated today.

6. Springfield: population 114,868

Springfield is located in the mostly flat plains of central Illinois. It serves as the state capital, and the state government is the city's largest employer. Springfield is also the final resting place of President Abraham Lincoln.

7. Peoria: population 112,883

Peoria was the site of the first European settlement in Illinois. French fur traders arrived in the Peoria River valley in 1673. French explorers built a small fort in 1680, which was the first European building in the Midwest. Today, it has many attractions, like the Peoria Zoo.

8. Elgin: population 112,456

Elgin was founded in 1835 and has been known as a center for dairy farming and as the leading producer of fine watches in the United States. It began to grow again in the 1990s with the arrival of the Grand Victoria riverboat casino.

9. Waukegan: population 87,729

The industries of Waukegan, located on the shore of Lake Michigan about 40 miles (64 km) north of Chicago, faced economic challenges in the last decades of the twentieth century. Today, the city is an attractive urban community focused on revitalizing, or bringing new life to, its waterfront.

10. Champaign: population 87,432

Champaign is perhaps best known as the home of the University of Illinois at Urbana-Champaign, which has more than forty-seven thousand students. The city also serves as a regional arts and culture hub.

Champaign

A tugboat moves cargo across the Illinois River.

Illinois's lakes and rivers are important both to the state's economy and to its wildlife. Commercial boats and barges commonly carry farm products and manufactured items to Illinois's ports. The goods are then shipped to the rest of the country and to countries all around the world. Pleasure and fishing boats also cruise Illinois's lakes and rivers. Meanwhile, many types of birds, fish, and other wildlife make their homes in or near the state's waterways.

Climate

Long, cold winters and hot, humid summers are common in northern Illinois. Almost every year, Chicago newspaper headlines report illnesses or deaths related to weather extremes.

In the winter, it is common for the temperature to dip well below 0 degrees Fahrenheit (–18 degrees Celsius). In the summer, it is equally common for the temperature to rise well above 90°F (32°C).

The Lake Michigan area can experience bitterly cold temperatures.

In the spring and early summer, the Mississippi and other rivers in Illinois sometimes overflow, causing floods in the lowlands along the rivers. In 1993, thousands of people in the western part of the state lost farms, homes, and businesses to floods. The flooding was the worst in Illinois history. Severe flooding

The Magnificent Mile

The Magnificent Mile in Chicago is one of the best-known downtown areas of any city in the world. It has something for people of all ages and interests. History buffs can admire the classic architecture of famous buildings such as the Tribune Tower (the former home of the *Chicago Tribune* newspaper) and the Wrigley Building. Those who love shopping will enjoy visiting a variety of high-end stores. Meanwhile, the Field Museum features forty million **artifacts** and scientific items, including mummies, the world's biggest dinosaur, and more.

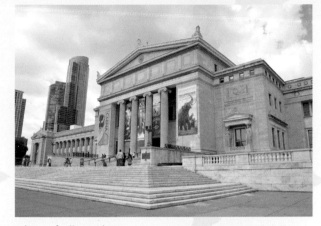

The Field Museum of Natural History in Chicago houses millions of specimens and artifacts.

The most popular attraction of all on the Magnificent Mile is the Navy Pier, which stretches out into Lake Michigan. Since 1995, the pier has hosted more than 180 million visitors. With dozens of shops and restaurants, the Navy Pier is a crowd pleaser. Families enjoy the IMAX Theatre and the Chicago Children's Museum, as well as a variety of rides. The most famous ride is the Centennial Wheel. With a peak height of nearly 200 feet (61 meters), the giant Ferris wheel offers breathtaking views of Chicago and Lake Michigan. Meanwhile, more than two hundred thousand theater lovers flock to the Chicago Shakespeare Theater each year to enjoy one of more than six hundred performances.

Highland Park faces
a major flood.

again occurred on the Mississippi and other rivers throughout central Illinois in 2008.

In the spring of 2013, 4 inches (10 centimeters) of rain fell around Galesburg in only thirty minutes, causing flooding that shut down Carl Sandberg College for several days. The water was high enough to cause desks to float, and up to thirty computers were damaged.

Severe thunderstorms are not uncommon in Illinois. With these storms comes the threat of tornadoes, especially in the spring and summer. A tornado is a swirling column of air that stretches from a storm cloud all the way to the ground. In a tornado, wind speeds can reach more than 200 miles per hour (320 kilometers per hour). Tornadoes can form quickly and can uproot trees and toss cars into the air.

Despite the sometimes harsh weather, the people of Illinois love to watch their state change with the seasons—the burst of new life in spring, the full bloom of summer, the glorious colors of fall, and the beauty of freshly fallen snow in winter.

Farm crops grow well in Illinois, but so do many wildflowers, grasses, and trees. Purple violets, lilies, bluebells, hyacinths, marsh marigolds, and other wildflowers sprinkle the roadsides and fields with color in spring and summer.

Some farmers in Illinois are in the process of planting trees for forests and wild grasses for prairies. Much of the land had been seriously eroded, or worn away, when it was farmed. One farmer described the gullies on his farm as deep enough to completely hold a car. Now this land is being managed to attract and feed wildlife. In addition, replanting the land with native grasses and trees helps prevent water pollution and flooding.

Setting Boundaries

The first Europeans to visit what is now Illinois were French missionary Jacques Marquette and explorer Louis Jolliet. In 1673, they traveled down the Mississippi River, seeking a route to China. They didn't find such a route, but they did claim the lands they passed along the way for France. In his journal, Marquette described the river in the Illinois area this way: "There are hardly any woods or mountains; The Islands are more beautiful, and are Covered with finer trees." He also described observing deer, cattle, swans, and "monstrous fish."

Later, the Illinois Territory became part of the land known as the Northwest Territory. The territory was organized by the US government in 1787. It included what are now Ohio, Michigan, Indiana, Illinois, and Wisconsin. However, the borders of Illinois have shifted over time.

Today, Lake Michigan forms a natural boundary to the east. The Mississippi River forms a natural boundary with Iowa and Missouri to the west. The Wabash and Ohio Rivers form much of the eastern and southern borders with Indiana and Kentucky. The rest of the border with Indiana stretches due north from where the Wabash River intersects the two states to Lake Michigan. The border between Illinois and Wisconsin runs due west from a point about 50 miles (80 km) north of Chicago.

The originally planned Illinois-Wisconsin border ran in a straight line from the southernmost tip of Lake Michigan to just south of where the Rock and Mississippi Rivers meet. That was the border set by an agreement called the Northwest Ordinance. If that boundary had stayed the case, then Chicago would have been part of Wisconsin! In 1818, as Illinois was petitioning to become a state, Illinois Territory's congressional delegate, Nathaniel Pope, convinced Congress to move the border 51 miles (82 km) north. That's how Chicago became a key part of Illinois. Additionally, moving the border gave Illinois 5.5 million acres (2.2 million ha) of rich farmland, as well as valuable shoreline along Lake Michigan.

Jacques Marquette and Louis Jolliet explored the Mississippi River in 1673, passing by what is now Illinois.

Flocks of Canada geese visit Illinois each year during their migration.

Illinois's Animals

A variety of animals and birds are native to Illinois. The white-tailed deer, the state's official animal, is the biggest animal in Illinois. Rabbits, squirrels, muskrats, skunks, raccoons, foxes, and mink scamper through the forests. Ducks, quail, grouse, and pheasant nest and feed along the state's waterways and in fields. Huge flocks of Canada geese darken the skies in the spring. They return from a winter spent farther south and stop in Illinois to build nests, lay eggs, and hatch their young. Thousands of Canada geese also live year-round throughout the state. The birds create problems by destroying crops and fouling lakes and ponds. However, they are a protected species and can be hunted only during specific times of the year. Many birds make their homes in the trees of Illinois. Cardinals and other songbirds sing out from the treetops. Bald eagles watch for prey while perched on high.

Animals in Danger

Some animals that were once common in Illinois have become extinct. The yellow-headed blackbird is in danger of disappearing from the state. Many of the marshes and wetlands that are the home of this beautiful bird have been drained. People have planted crops and built houses and factories on the drained land.

Other animals are in danger of dying out. Among them are fish, including several species of sturgeon and chub. Types of turtles, snakes,

Some types of turtles are endangered in Illinois, including the Blanding's turtle, shown here.

and salamanders could also completely disappear. Pollution and the loss of forests have put species of hawks, owls, songbirds, and shorebirds, as well as several small woods and prairie animals, at risk of losing their natural homes. Many other animals and numerous plants are endangered in Illinois and are likely to become extinct unless people make a strong effort to save them.

The Great State of Illinois

Illinois ranks right in the middle of all states in terms of size. Illinois is the twenty-fifth largest state and covers 57,914 square miles (149,997 square kilometers). Within that area, the state possesses a rich and varied geography. It boasts forests and fields, rivers and lakes, and cliffs and canyons. Residents take advantage of cold winters and hot summers. Visitors come to see big cities and small towns. It's not surprising that more than twelve million people choose to call Illinois their home.

What Lives in Illinois?

Illinois is known for its crops of pumpkins.

Slippery elm

Sunflowers

Flora

Corn Corn, the top cash crop in Illinois, covers about 12 million acres (5 million ha) across the state. In 2016, Illinois ranked second among all states in growing corn, producing more than two billion bushels. Most of the corn is sold for grain and livestock feed. About one-quarter goes to making corn **ethanol** for use in gasoline.

Pumpkins Illinois is by far the top pumpkin-producing state in the United States. It grows more than twice as many pounds of pumpkins as the next state, California. In 2015, Illinois farmers grew 317.9 million pounds (144 million kilograms) of pumpkins.

Slippery Elm The white oak may be the state tree, but the slippery elm is the most common tree across the state. It can grow to a height of more than 60 feet (18 m). The inner bark of the tree can be used to treat a variety of health conditions.

Soybeans Illinois ranks as the nation's leading soybean producer. Between 2014 and 2017, the state produced more than six hundred million bushels each year. Soybeans are the state's second-biggest cash crop, behind corn. Most soybeans are processed for use in animal feed. Some are made into products such as soy milk and tofu.

Sunflowers Sunflowers thrive in prairie states such as Illinois. The bright yellow flowers grow 5 to 8 feet (1.5 to 2.4 m) tall and bloom in midsummer. The plant got its name because the flowers always turn toward the sun. In addition to being pretty, some kinds of sunflowers are used for food, seeds, and oil.

Fauna

Bluegill Members of the sunfish family, bluegills are named for the blue color around their mouth and gills. Schoolchildren across Illinois selected the bluegill as the state fish in 1986. Bluegills may not be large—around 9 inches (23 cm) long and less than 1 pound (0.5 kg)—but they are noted for their fighting spirit.

Bluegill

Bobcats Once a threatened species in Illinois, bobcats have made a big comeback since the early 1990s. Today, as many as five thousand are estimated to live throughout the state. Bobcats are about twice the size of common house cats and may weight up to about 40 pounds (18 kg).

Cardinal The cardinal is the state bird of Illinois. The male cardinal is famous for its bright red color and ring of black around the beak. These songbirds can live up to fifteen years in the wild.

Monarch Butterfly Illinois named the monarch butterfly as the state insect in 1975. A third-grade student first suggested the idea, and other schoolchildren joined the lobbying effort. Illinois lies on one of the key migration paths as the butterflies travel back and forth from Mexico to the northern United States. Illinois is working to protect the butterfly, whose numbers are falling.

Bobcat

Pigs Illinois ranks fourth among all states in pork production. In 2018, there were more than five million pigs in the state. Hogs represent the most important livestock product in the entire state. The pork industry contributes $1.8 billion to the state's economy each year and accounts for more than ten thousand jobs.

A pig farm in Illinois

Cahokia Mounds State Historic Site preserves the ceremonial mounds built by ancient people who made Illinois their home.

2 The History of Illinois

Illinois celebrated its two-hundredth anniversary as a state in 2018. A lot has happened over those two hundred years. The state has grown and changed. But it's important to remember that a critical part of Illinois's history took place long before it was a state. People lived there centuries before European explorers and settlers arrived. In fact, to truly understand Illinois, we have to begin thousands of years ago and thousands of miles away.

The frozen plains of Siberia in northern Asia are a key part of Illinois's early history. Scientists believe that between ten thousand and thirty thousand years ago, the Bering Sea—the stretch of water between Alaska and eastern Siberia—did not exist. Sea levels were lower then, and land that is now under the Bering Sea was above water, creating a land bridge between the two continents. Most anthropologists (scientists who study different cultures, including ancient cultures) think a few brave, strong people crossed that bridge. If this is true, the many Native tribes that spread across the Americas are the descendants of those adventurers.

The earliest people to live in the area now called Illinois were **nomadic** groups that moved

FAST FACT

Four US Presidents have strong ties to Illinois. Ronald Reagan (1981–1989) was born there. Both Abraham Lincoln (1861–1865) and Barack Obama (2009–2017) represented Illinois in Congress. Ulysses S. Grant (1869–1877) had a home in the state.

from place to place hunting large game. Later, people who lived in the region hunted smaller game and gathered wild grains and edible roots, bulbs, berries, and nuts. Eventually, the region's Natives began to grow grain instead of gathering it where it grew wild. They ground the grain into coarse flour for cooking and baking.

The Ancient Illinoisans

Over time, ancient people in what is now Illinois learned more about the food plants whose seeds they collected and scattered each year. They learned where the plants grew best and decided to stay in these areas year-round. About three thousand years ago, they began building permanent settlements, mostly in river valleys.

The ancient Illinoisans, even before they built year-round settlements, buried some members of their groups in earthen **mounds**. Over the centuries, they built larger and more complex mounds. By about 100 BCE, mound building had become an important part of the culture of many peoples living in the American Midwest.

Mississippian Culture

In about 700 CE, people in Illinois began growing corn as a main food source. It was a more reliable source of food than other crops. The cultivation of corn led to growth in the population and to the development of a distinctive culture. Because most of the people lived along the Mississippi or other rivers flowing into the Mississippi, the culture is called the Mississippian culture.

In the Mississippian culture, small villages surrounded large towns or cities. At the center of most towns and cities was a large, flat mound with a temple or a leader's home built on top. The largest of the Mississippian cities

was **Cahokia**, in southwestern Illinois. The city served as a cultural center for centuries. About twenty thousand people lived in Cahokia when the city was at its peak.

Over the next 250 years, Cahokia's population declined. By 1400, very few people lived in Cahokia and in other large Mississippian villages in present-day Illinois. This may have been because the climate was getting colder, which led to poor harvests. Overpopulation, disease, and invasion might have also added to the problems.

The Arrival of Europeans

In 1673, the French government in New France (part of present-day Canada) was looking for new trade routes. Louis Jolliet and Jacques Marquette were chosen to explore the river that the Algonquian-speakers called Misisipi, or "big river." They wanted to see if the river stretched west to the Pacific Ocean. Louis Jolliet was a French Canadian who had been exploring the Great Lakes region for New France. Jacques Marquette was a French priest who had worked and lived among the Native Americans and could speak a number of Native American languages. In May 1673, Marquette and Jolliet launched canoes at the northern edge of Lake Michigan and began their journey southward.

The Native People

When Europeans first arrived in the Great Lakes region, two major Native American tribes lived in what would later be known as Illinois. The first group, known to the French explorers as the Illinois, or Illiniwek, was a collection of several independent Native American tribes. This collection of tribes shared a language and customs. The tribes included the Kaskaskia, Cahokia, Tamaroa, Peoria, and Michigamea. The second group was known as the Miami tribe, and they lived in villages located south and west of Lake Michigan. The Shawnee and Chickasaw lived in small parts of the southern region, and the Dakota and the Ho-Chunk populated the northern borders with what is now Wisconsin.

Both the Illinois and Miami tribes spoke a language in the Algonquian language family called Miami-Illinois. Although they pronounced some words differently, Miami and Illinois peoples could easily understand one another. They made canoes of hollowed-out logs and used dogs as pack animals to transport their goods. (There were no horses until European settlers brought them.)

As Europeans arrived, the Illinois caught diseases that the explorers and settlers brought with them. The Illinois also had to deal with wars against the Iroquois tribe, which was expanding into the area. During the 1700s and early 1800s, the Illinois

This map shows where some of Illinois's Native American tribes lived in the late seventeenth century.

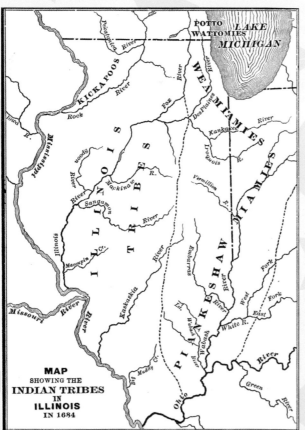

MAP
SHOWING THE
INDIAN TRIBES
IN
ILLINOIS
IN 1684

had less and less territory, and the Miami tribe moved eastward. Many members of the Illinois decided to go to what is now Kansas. Other tribes then moved to the Illinois area to take over that land. These newly arrived tribes included the Fox (Mesquakie), Ioway, Kickapoo, Mascouten, Piankashaw, Potawatomi, Sauk, Shawnee, Wea, and Winnebago. Most of these tribes disappeared from Illinois by about the mid-nineteenth century, either through warfare or because the federal government forced them to move to other territories.

A wigwam stands at the Grove National Historic Landmark in Glenview.

Spotlight on the Illinois

Houses: The Illinois moved between three types of settlements during the year. During the spring and early summer, they raised corn and lived in mat-covered longhouses near rivers. In June and July, they built hunting camps in the prairies using bark-covered lodges. For the winter, they moved to areas along the bottoms of dry rivers that were good locations for hunting. They lived in oval, mat-covered lodges called wigwams.

Clothing: The early Illinois wore clothing made from the skins and hair of deer, bison, and other animals they hunted. Over time, the Illinois began to wear clothes made of wool and other fabrics instead.

Music: The main Illinois musical instruments included the drum, rattle, and flute. Drums were made from large ceramic pots with an opening covered by buckskin. Rattles were fashioned from hollow gourds that contained glass beads and were attached to wooden handles. Flutes were carved from wood.

Children: Illinois children did chores but also enjoyed playing with toys such as child-sized bows and arrows and corn husk dolls. Illinois teenagers also liked to play a version of lacrosse and other sports.

Marquette and Jolliet paddled along the shores of Lake Michigan and then traveled down rivers in what is today Wisconsin. They eventually reached the Mississippi River. They followed it as far south as present-day Arkansas. They also traveled north, along the Illinois River. A year later, Marquette returned to the banks of the Illinois River to establish a mission (a religious settlement) at a Native American village called Kaskaskia, which later became the town of Utica.

The French claimed the area that Marquette and Jolliet explored, naming it Illinois, after the Native Americans who lived there. In the early 1700s, the French considered Illinois part of their province of Louisiana—a vast area that included nearly the entire middle section of North America. The first permanent European settlement in Illinois was established in the town of Cahokia in 1699.

Despite their differences, Europeans and Native Americans traded with each other. Native Americans exchanged animal skins for the Europeans' metal tools, horses, and guns. As more settlers came and took more land, tensions increased.

The arrival of more Europeans took its toll on the land. Settlers chopped down forests and hunted animals for food and their skins. Native Americans could no longer find the animals they needed for food. In self-defense, they learned to use their horses and guns to fight back against the Europeans. More European colonists kept coming, however, and the Native Americans were fighting a hopeless battle.

The European settlers also fought each other. During the French and Indian War (1754–1763), the British and French competed for control of North America, and both were aided by Native American allies. The British won the

This painting by artist Edwin Willard Deming shows a battle during the French and Indian War.

war and gained control of Illinois and most other French territory in North America east of the Mississippi River. Despite this, most white people in Illinois at that time were French.

Illinois and the American Revolution

By the 1770s, many colonists along the eastern coast of North America wanted to break free from British control. The original thirteen colonies approved the Declaration of Independence on July 4, 1776, but freedom did not come easily. First, the colonists had to fight and win the American Revolution.

Most battles were fought in the eastern colonies, but some fighting took place in Illinois. The most important battle in Illinois was on July 4, 1778. American forces led by George Rogers Clark captured the British forts at Kaskaskia, Cahokia, and several other small

towns. In his journal, Clark wrote, "In the evening, we got within a few miles of the town [Kaskaskia], where we lay until near dark ... In a very little time we had complete possession." Clark claimed all the territory north of the Ohio River as part of the newly formed United States. Clark's victory at Kaskaskia also persuaded local French residents to fight on the American side.

The Illinois Territory

When the American colonists eventually won their independence from Britain in 1783, almost all the land between the former colonies and the Mississippi River became part of the new United States. The area north of the Ohio River, including Illinois, was called the Northwest Territory. In 1800, the part of the Northwest Territory that included present-day Illinois was renamed the Indiana Territory. Nine years later, the district split. Part of the district became the Illinois Territory, which included present-day Illinois, Wisconsin, and parts of Michigan and Minnesota.

In the early 1800s, Americans of European descent started moving into present-day Illinois in large numbers. The new land was good for farming, so they built cabins and chopped through the tough prairie sod (grass-covered soil) to plant crops. Many items these settlers had taken for granted in their previous homes were not available. They had to make most of their own goods or

In 1830, Abraham Lincoln's family moved to this log cabin in Macon County.

do without them. Abraham Lincoln's family built a cabin in Illinois in 1830.

Illinois officially became the twenty-first state on December 3, 1818. By 1830, the state's population had grown to more than 160,000 people. As more settlers arrived, the remaining Native Americans were forced to move west. Some Native Americans refused to leave their homelands. In 1832, Black Hawk, a leader among the Sauk and Fox tribes,

In 1832, Native American leader Black Hawk tried to win back tribal land from white settlers.

tried to take back tribal land in northern Illinois and Wisconsin. He and his warriors fought bravely, but they were badly outnumbered and were quickly defeated. President Andrew Jackson sent Black Hawk and his son Whirling Thunder around the country as "trophies" of war. The two men showed incredible dignity in the face of such terrible treatment. Later, Black Hawk returned to his people on a **reservation** in Iowa, where he wrote his autobiography.

Throughout the period, the United States government signed pacts and treaties with Native tribes. The government took away the lands on which the Native Americans had always lived and gave them other land farther west. But as European American settlers moved toward the Pacific coast, many of those treaties were broken.

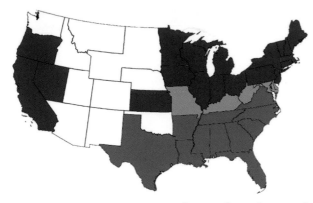

The Civil War

By the mid-1800s, tensions between the Northern and Southern states were rising. The Northern states flourished as a result of manufacturing, trade, and mass production. The Southern states thrived by farming cash crops, such as cotton, tobacco, and rice. Southern plantation owners relied on black slaves to raise their crops, and slavery was a basic part of Southern life.

Areas in dark blue mark the Union during the Civil War. Areas in red are the Confederacy. Light blue states were part of the Union but allowed slavery.

As the United States grew, adding territory in the West, the nation became divided over the issue of slavery. The Northern states were "free states." Slavery had been abolished or was never legal in these states. The free states wanted slavery to be illegal in most of the new states that were added as the nation grew. In addition, some people opposed slavery on moral grounds. They wanted slavery to be abolished throughout the nation.

The Southern states were "slave states." Not only did they consider it a right to own slaves, they also tended to vote together in Congress and did not want to lose influence in the national government as new states were added. To help hold on to their political power, the slave states wanted slavery to be legal in western territories. At the least, they wanted the citizens of the territories to vote on whether their new state would be a free state or a slave state. By the spring of 1861, eleven Southern states had broken away from the Union (the United States) and formed the Confederate States of America. The Civil War had begun.

Illinois was a free state and was one of the states that fought for the Union against the Confederacy during the Civil War. More than 250,000 Illinoisans fought in the Union army. Nearly thirty-five thousand of these soldiers died in the war. One Illinois soldier who fought in the war was Ulysses S. Grant. He volunteered in Springfield and rose in rank to become the head of the Union army. A few years after the war ended, in 1868, Grant was elected president of the United States.

In 1858, Abraham Lincoln (*left*) had a series of debates with Stephen A. Douglas (*right*) during the race for a US Senate seat.

Abraham Lincoln was a central figure before and during the Civil War. Having studied and practiced law in Illinois, Lincoln set his sights on a political career. While running for the US Senate in 1858, Lincoln participated in many debates in the state against Stephen A. Douglas and argued against slavery. He lost the Senate election to Douglas, but in 1860, Lincoln was elected president of the United States. He was reelected in 1864.

Lincoln believed that the Union must be held together. In a famous speech on June 17, 1858, during the Senate race, he said: "A house divided against itself cannot stand. I believe this government cannot endure permanently half slave and half free. I do not expect the Union to be dissolved; I do not expect the house to

Abraham Lincoln's burial site in Springfield brings visitors from all over.

fall; but I do expect it will cease to be divided. It will become all one thing, or all the other."

He led the country through the Civil War and is often thought of as one of America's greatest leaders. However, Lincoln did not get to continue his leadership after the Union victory. On April 14, 1865, only a few days after the main Confederate army surrendered, Lincoln was shot while watching a play in Washington, DC. He died the next day. On April 21, a funeral train left Washington, DC, and made its way through 180 cities and seven states before arriving in Springfield, Illinois. Lincoln was buried there on May 4. A few months after Lincoln's death, the US Constitution was changed. The Thirteenth Amendment officially ended slavery throughout the United States.

Illinoisans are extremely proud that Abraham Lincoln spent most of his adult life in Illinois. Like many people around the world, they admire Lincoln's principles. It is no surprise, then, that Illinoisans adopted "Land of Lincoln" as the state's slogan.

The Rise of Chicago

In 1803, the US Army established Fort Dearborn near present-day Chicago. Soon, European American settlers started coming to the area. In 1812, Native Americans attacked and burned Fort Dearborn. The fort was rebuilt four years later, but few people returned to the settlement until the Sauk tribe's leader, Black Hawk, was defeated in the early 1830s. From then on, the city grew rapidly. New canals connected Chicago, along with other growing cities, to the rivers that fed into the Mississippi. Railroads were built across the continent. Many of these train lines met in Chicago. The canals and the railroads helped

This image shows Chicago in the 1860s, before the Great Chicago Fire of 1871 caused terrible destruction.

Chicago become an important port and industrial center in the mid-1800s.

But Chicago almost did not survive into the 1900s. On the night of October 8, 1871, a fire started in or near Patrick and Catherine O'Leary's barn in Chicago and spread through the city. Legend says that a cow kicked over a lantern, but no one knows for sure how the fire started. The Great Chicago Fire destroyed nearly every home and business in the city. More than three hundred people died, and eighteen thousand buildings were destroyed, leaving many people homeless. The people of Chicago fought back, and soon the city was on the rise again. One of the buildings to survive the fire was the Historic Water Tower. It still stands today, surrounded by soaring skyscrapers, and serves as a symbol of Chicago's strong spirit.

The Historic Water Tower (*center*) survived the Great Chicago Fire.

Industrialization

During the 1800s, many new industries were born in Illinois. Many of these companies still exist today. Cyrus McCormick invented a reaper that helped farmers harvest huge fields of crops quickly. John Deere invented a steel plow to replace old wooden and iron plows. The steel plows worked better than wooden ones in the tough prairie soil and lasted longer. Farmers from Illinois and neighboring

For decades, cattle and hogs were processed at the Union Stock Yard in Chicago.

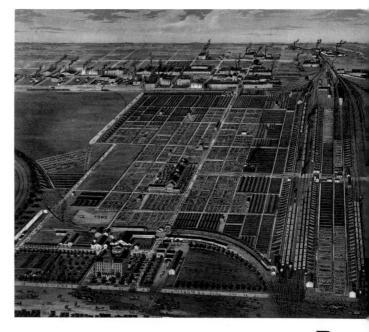

Make Your Own Pumpkin Volcano

Illinois is by far the top pumpkin-producing state in the United States. Create your own pumpkin volcano to learn about chemical reactions!

Supplies

- A medium-sized pumpkin
- Pumpkin carving tools
- Vinegar
- Dish detergent
- Food coloring
- 1 tablespoon of baking soda

Directions

1. Cut the top off the pumpkin and hollow out the inside.
2. Fill the pumpkin about halfway with vinegar.
3. Add a squirt of dish detergent and a few drops of food coloring or liquid watercolors to the vinegar and stir the mixture.
4. Measure out a heaping tablespoon of baking soda and dump it into the pumpkin. Stir it in.
5. Stand back and watch the bubbly mixture erupt out the top of the pumpkin and spill over the sides.

The pH scale is a scale used by scientists to label acids and bases. When acids like vinegar combine with bases like baking soda, the two react with each other. Together, they make carbon dioxide gas. The result is an eruption!

states sent cattle and hogs to be slaughtered, or killed, in stockyards near Chicago, and Gustavus Swift opened a meat-processing plant in the area.

Aaron Montgomery Ward began a mail-order business. He was so successful that Richard Sears and Alvah Roebuck did the same thing. Both companies opened large department stores that generations of shoppers loved to visit. Although Ward's now only does business online, Sears still has many department stores.

Chicago's factories were so successful that by 1890, Illinois was the third-largest manufacturing state in the nation. Products included farm machinery, clothing, steel products, food products, and more.

Sears opened its first department store in Illinois in the late 1800s.

World War I and World War II

In 1914, World War I broke out in Europe. The United States entered the war in 1917, joining Great Britain and France in fighting Germany and Austria-Hungary. Illinoisans contributed to the war by enlisting in the armed forces and by working in factories to produce war materials.

In the 1930s, the nation sank into the **Great Depression**. Thousands of banks closed and businesses failed. Many people lost their farms or their jobs, and some lost their homes. Millions of people across the country were unemployed. It was a time of great hardship.

By the end of the 1930s, the world was drawn into World War II. In Europe, Adolf Hitler's Nazi German troops stormed across neighboring countries. In Asia, Japan conquered parts of China and numerous territories that at the time were European colonies. The United States entered the war in late 1941, after the Japanese bombed Pearl Harbor, a US naval base in Hawaii.

FAST FACT

Illinois has always been a national leader in women's rights. In 1913, Illinois became the first state east of the Mississippi River to give women the right to vote at the state level. In 1919, the US Senate passed the Nineteenth Amendment. This amendment gave women nationwide the right to vote. Illinois, along with Wisconsin and Michigan, ratified the amendment within a week.

Famous People from Illinois

Jane Addams

Gwendolyn Brooks

Jane Addams

Born in Cedarville in 1860, Addams founded the world's first settlement house. Settlement houses provided services for immigrants and needy families. Addams is considered the founder of the social work profession. She won the Nobel Peace Prize in 1931.

Black Hawk

In 1832, Black Hawk led one thousand Sauks, Foxes, and Kickapoos in battle against the Illinois militia. The Native Americans hoped to reclaim land in Illinois that had been taken from them through an unfair treaty. In the end, Black Hawk surrendered. He spent time as a prisoner and later died in Iowa.

Gwendolyn Brooks

Born in Kansas, Brooks moved to Chicago at a young age. A noted poet, author, and teacher, she won the Pulitzer Prize for Poetry in 1950 for her book *Annie Allen*. She became the first African American to receive this honor. Her poetry books for children include the classic *Bronzeville Boys and Girls*.

Miles Davis

An Illinois native, Davis was one of the top jazz musicians of the twentieth century. He was a noted trumpet player and composer. His career spanned five decades. Over that time, he worked with many of the country's top jazz musicians. In 2006, he was inducted into the Rock and Roll Hall of Fame.

Walt Disney

Born in Hermosa, a neighborhood of Chicago, in 1901, Disney created Mickey Mouse and other memorable Disney characters. He won thirty-two

Academy Awards for his movies. He created the Disneyland and Walt Disney World theme parks. In 2017, Disney parks around the world drew an estimated 150 million visitors.

Walt Disney

Enrico Fermi

Fermi directed a series of experiments in Chicago that led to the first controlled nuclear chain reaction in December 1942. He went on to help lead the Manhattan Project. This was the project that developed the atomic bomb. He won the Nobel Prize in Physics in 1938.

Betty Friedan

A leader in the women's rights movement, she cofounded the National Organization for Women. Her book *The Feminine Mystique* encouraged women to explore career options outside of their traditional roles. She was born in 1921 in Peoria.

Ernest Hemingway

Born in Cicero, Illinois, in 1899, Hemingway was one of the best-known novelists of the twentieth century. In 1953, he won the Pulitzer Prize for his book *The Old Man and the Sea*. In 1954, he won the Nobel Prize for Literature.

Abraham Lincoln

Although born in Kentucky, Lincoln rose to fame as a lawyer and legislator in Illinois before becoming the nation's sixteenth president. He led the Union through the Civil War. He was **assassinated** just as the war was ending.

Cyrus McCormick

McCormick is credited as one of the inventors of the mechanical reaping machine. He opened a factory in Chicago in 1847 to manufacture his machines. His company was a huge success.

Cyrus McCormick

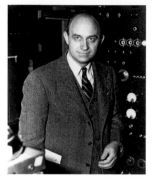

Enrico Fermi and fellow scientists at the University of Chicago did groundbreaking research on atomic energy in the 1940s.

Factories and farms scrambled to provide supplies needed by the armed forces, including weapons, tanks, trucks, ships, planes, food, and uniforms. The war helped to ease the unemployment of the Great Depression. Thousands of men and women from Illinois served in the armed forces. Many more served by working in factories and on farms as the economy had to ramp up to produce the products needed to supply the troops.

The war brought about major advances in atomic research. In 1942, under the direction of Enrico Fermi, an Italian American physicist, scientists at the University of Chicago set off the first human-made nuclear chain reaction. A nuclear chain reaction involves the release of tremendous energy from the nucleus (center) of an atom, the building block of matter. More research led to the creation of the atomic bomb. The United States dropped two atomic bombs on Japanese cities, which helped bring World War II to an end in 1945. Nuclear research also led to peaceful uses of nuclear power for power plants that make electricity. Today, the Chicago area remains a leader in atomic and nuclear research.

Modern Illinois

During the second half of the twentieth century, Illinoisans faced many problems. Increasing costs forced many farmers to sell their land to large corporations or to land developers. Land that was once rich farmland was cleared to make way for homes, businesses, and factories.

Urban areas also faced rough times. Over the course of the 1900s, cities had grown more crowded, leading to increases in racial tension, poverty, crime, and drug problems. In the mid- and late 1900s, many people and businesses moved out of the cities and into the

The Chicago International Film Festival

Lights! Camera! Action! Every year since 1964, movie lovers from all over the world have flocked to the Chicago International Film Festival. It is the longest-running film festival in North America.

In recent years, famous actors such as Patrick Stewart and Vanessa Redgrave have made appearances, and top new films have been screened. At many of the screenings, attendees can meet directors, producers, writers, and cast members.

Each year, the festival showcases a wide range of feature films, documentaries, and short films. Films include Oscar contenders, as well as award winners from other top international film festivals. The festival also spotlights certain categories each year. Through the years, the festival has contributed to the "discovery" of noted directors such as Martin Scorsese (*Goodfellas* and many others) and horror film master John Carpenter (the *Halloween* series and others).

Each year, the Chicago International Film Festival draws some of the movie industry's top directors and actors.

Cinema/Chicago, the nonprofit organization that presents the festival, also runs cultural and educational events throughout the year. Their goal is to encourage better communication between people of diverse cultures, using films as the starting point.

For many years, the Cabrini-Green low-income housing project in Chicago served as an example of big-city poverty. It has since been torn down.

expanding suburbs. Inner cities had less money to support their schools and for upkeep of older neighborhoods. Inner-city residents also had fewer opportunities to find good jobs.

Illinoisans today are working hard to solve those problems and create a bright future. Immigrants from all over the world, especially from Latin America and Asia, have moved to Illinois. They are helping to make Illinois a diverse and successful state.

The Bicentennial

The year 2018 marked the two hundredth anniversary of Illinois's statehood. The state created a bicentennial flag, coin, and license plate to mark the occasion. A series of special events throughout the year included plays emphasizing history at the state's popular Theatre in the Park from May through September 2018 in Petersburg. Down on the Farm events in Danville in June 2018 spotlighted agricultural history and rural life in Illinois. Meanwhile, a statewide media campaign celebrated Illinois's influence on the world.

In August 2018, the state celebrated the two hundredth anniversary of its constitution and dedicated a new Bicentennial Plaza in Springfield next to the Governor's Mansion. A special event in Chicago on December 3 marked the date Illinois was admitted to the Union as the twenty-first state. The event featured Illinois celebrities from the sports and entertainment world. A mix of historical videos and live entertainment highlighted the giant birthday party. A grand finale spotlighted Chicago's central role in the jazz and blues movements in the United States.

Throughout its two hundred years as a state, Illinois has provided more than its share of leaders in politics, industry, sports, and the arts. Four US presidents have deep ties to Illinois, along with many other important national politicians. Its major sports teams have won more than twenty-five national championships. Many high-profile actors, musicians, and artists hail from Illinois, and Chicago serves as a Midwestern center for music, theater, and other arts. The state has long been a leader in the agricultural industry as well.

Even as it celebrates its rich history, Illinois also looks ahead. The state is filled with resources. Illinois's most important resource, however, is its people. Illinoisans continue to make history.

Chicago is a bustling city, and people from all walks of life make a home there.

3 Who Lives in Illinois?

Lots of different types of people make Illinois their home. As the nation's fifth most populous state, Illinois claims residents that represent diverse ethnicities, languages, and ages. People who identify as non-Hispanic white make up about 61 percent of the population, followed by 17 percent Hispanic residents and 15 percent black residents. Nearly one in four residents (22.7 percent) speak a language other than English at home.

Illinoisans live in cities, suburbs, towns, and farms. They work in a wide variety of jobs. Some families have lived in Illinois for generations. Others are newcomers to the state.

Rural Illinoisans

Farm life in Illinois today is much different from when the first settlers came. Today, most farms are fully computerized, and modern machinery makes farm life easier than it used to be. However, farm families still work hard. Children on farms often get up at about 5:00 a.m. to do chores before getting on the school bus.

FAST FACT
Many famous movies are set in Illinois, and some were filmed there. Movies like *Home Alone*, *The Breakfast Club*, *Ferris Bueller's Day Off*, *Sixteen Candles*, *The Blues Brothers*, *Batman Begins*, *The Sting*, *Risky Business*, and many others have ties to Illinois. Movies filmed in the state give Illinoisans a chance to appear as extras.

In today's connected world, Illinois farmers and their families often have similar lifestyles to city people.

Life in Towns and Cities

Modern equipment makes life easier for farmers.

Although more than three-quarters of Illinois is still made up of farm fields, most Illinoisans live in the towns and small cities sprinkled throughout the state. Each place has its own history, style, and culture. Galena in northwestern Illinois is a beautiful, old, historic town. Carbondale claims the nationally recognized Southern Illinois University. Decatur, in the middle of Illinois, is a center for business and industry and an urban hub for the surrounding farming areas. Some cities in Illinois are part of a bigger metropolitan area, which has a large central city surrounded by smaller cities or towns.

Every ten years, the US government counts the number of people living in the United States. This count is called the census. In between, census estimates are issued. According to the 2017 census estimate, Illinois is home to about 12.8 million people.

The biggest metropolitan area in Illinois is Chicago. People who live there refer to the city and surrounding suburbs as Chicagoland. Chicago has about 2.7 million people, making it the third-largest city in the country. Like many large cities, Chicago has interesting restaurants, creative theater, and museums filled with fascinating exhibits.

Illinois has more to offer than just big cities. Small towns like Galena are full of history and charm.

Chicago is also known for its beautiful lakefront, its stunning architecture, and for being the home of Second City, a renowned sketch comedy troupe. In different seasons, people can go hiking, biking, canoeing, kayaking, swimming, sailing, and cross-country skiing, all in downtown Chicago. Bustling with activity, many parts of Chicago are great places to live and work as well as to visit.

However, not all parts of the city are quite so well off. In poor neighborhoods, many people have to deal with problems such as high unemployment and crime rates, overcrowding, and poverty. Some public schools in Chicago are very crowded. They do not have enough money to provide textbooks or even qualified teachers for all their students.

To address problems such as these, students in some of Chicago's high schools have been working with parents and community groups to improve their education. They did a yearlong study to find out why many students in the local public schools do not complete high school. They visited successful urban schools in other cities to learn effective ways to teach and motivate students. The students produced a report that they presented to the city. Their report outlined how they could work with the community and the school system to help more students graduate from high school and go on to college.

Many of Chicago's suburbs offer the benefits of both a large city and a smaller town. Many people like living in the suburbs because they can live in a quiet and peaceful area but still be close to the liveliness of the city.

FAST FACT
The University of Chicago ranked as the third-best university nationwide (tied with three other universities) in the *US News & World Report*'s 2019 rankings. Northwestern University was tied for tenth place with Maryland's Johns Hopkins University.

Chicago's public schools have faced challenges, but community groups work hard to make sure that all students get a high-quality education.

Illinois's Biggest Colleges and Universities

(Enrollment numbers are from *US News and World Report* 2019 college rankings.)

University of Illinois at Urbana-Champaign

DePaul University

Northwestern University

1. University of Illinois at Urbana-Champaign
(33,955 undergraduate students)

2. University of Illinois at Chicago
(19,448 undergraduate students)

3. Illinois State University, Normal
(18,330 undergraduate students)

4. DePaul University, Chicago
(14,816 undergraduate students)

5. Northern Illinois University, DeKalb
(13,454 undergraduate students)

6. Loyola University Chicago
(11,420 undergraduate students)

7. Southern Illinois University Edwardsville
(11,402 undergraduate students)

8. Southern Illinois University Carbondale
(10,987 undergraduate students)

9. Northwestern University, Evanston
(8,278 undergraduate students)

10. Western Illinois University, Macomb
(7,599 undergraduate students)

Religious Beliefs

Illinoisans come from many different religious backgrounds. The largest religious groups are Protestants and Catholics. The state is also home to many Jews, Muslims, Hindus, and Buddhists. Some Illinoisans choose not to be part of any organized religion.

Illinois is important in the history of the Church of Jesus Christ of Latter Day Saints, or the Mormons. In 1839, founder Joseph Smith and his followers settled in Commerce, Illinois. Smith renamed the city Nauvoo. The city's population grew to about twelve thousand. Still, the Mormons were often persecuted for their beliefs. Smith was murdered in jail in Carthage, Illinois, in June 1844. Less than two years later, Brigham Young led the Mormons out of Nauvoo to a new settlement in Utah. Today, the city of Nauvoo attracts many visitors who come to see historic Mormon sites.

This reconstructed Mormon temple recalls the years the Mormons spent in Nauvoo before moving to Utah.

Protecting Native American Culture

Native Americans make up less than 1 percent of the population of Illinois. Despite their small

Celebrities from Illinois

Chance the Rapper

A Chicago native, Chance is a noted rapper, songwriter, and actor. He is known for giving back to his home city. Chance started a nonprofit called SocialWorks to support young people in Chicago through funding for schools and other programs.

Sandra Cisneros

Sandra Cisneros is an award-winning writer who was born in Chicago in 1954. After studying English at Loyola University in Chicago, she attended the prestigious Iowa Writers' Workshop for her master's degree. Her books include *The House on Mango Street* and *A House of My Own*.

Harrison Ford

From Han Solo to Indiana Jones, this Chicago native has created some of Hollywood's most beloved characters. Ford has appeared in dozens of films since he became a professional actor in the 1960s.

Jennifer Hudson

Jennifer Hudson

A former *American Idol* contestant, Chicagoan Jennifer Hudson has since won Grammy Awards for singing, an Academy Award for acting, and many other honors. Hudson mentors singers on *The Voice* and created a charitable organization in memory of family members who were killed in 2008.

Bill Murray

An early *Saturday Night Live* cast member, Bill Murray was born in Wilmette. He got his start acting with the world-famous Second City comedy troupe in Chicago. He has starred in dozens of movies in both comedic and dramatic roles.

Michelle Obama

Michelle Obama was born in Chicago in 1964. The former First Lady of the United States is a lawyer and writer. As First Lady, she advocated for education, nutrition, and other issues. Her memoir, *Becoming*, was released in 2018 and broke sales records.

Michelle Obama

Shonda Rhimes

Shonda Rhimes was born in University Park. She is a talented producer and writer who has created several hit television shows, including *Grey's Anatomy* and *Scandal*. In addition to her television shows, Rhimes has written a best-selling book.

Dwyane Wade

Dwyane Wade was born in Chicago in 1982. He grew up playing basketball and was drafted into the NBA in 2003 by the Miami Heat. Wade has helped the team win three NBA championships. He has also received many awards, including the 2010 NBA All-Star MVP award.

Mo Willems

Betty White

The Emmy Award–winning actress, born in Oak Park, has enjoyed a television career spanning more than seven decades. White first gained fame on sitcoms like *The Mary Tyler Moore Show* and *The Golden Girls*.

Mo Willems

A Des Plaines native, Willems has delighted young readers for many years with zany characters like Pigeon and Knuffle Bunny. Willems's books have won some of the biggest awards in children's literature.

numbers, Native Americans have a strong presence in the state. For decades, they have worked to fight stereotypes and give people accurate information about their different tribes, their cultures, and their traditions. For example, many college athletic teams are named after Native American tribes or chiefs. The team names were not meant to offend anyone, but the team symbols and mascots often failed to show respect for Native cultures.

Native Americans and others at the University of Illinois at Champaign-Urbana brought national attention to this issue. Over the years, athletic events at the school featured the university mascot, Chief Illiniwek. The mascot would do a dance to raise team spirit. That presented several problems. The Illinois Natives (also called the Illiniwek) were Algonquian. But the mascot's costume was based on the clothing of Plains tribes. Even more important, traditional dances are sacred rituals in Native American cultures. They are not meant to entertain crowds at athletic events. Chief Illiniwek's dance offended many people.

In 2007, after numerous meetings with Native groups, faculty, students, and alumni, the University of Illinois retired Chief Illiniwek as the school's mascot. As of 2018, the university was still discussing what to choose as a new mascot.

African American Heritage

The first African American town to be incorporated in the United States was Brooklyn, Illinois. Brooklyn, which was also called Lovejoy, had its beginnings in the 1820s. Black slaves escaped to the area and set up a community of farmers and craftspeople. Brooklyn, Illinois,

Chicago is famous for its deep-dish pizza, but you don't have to travel to the Windy City to enjoy it. The key is the dough. Here is a simple recipe for making a deep-dish pizza.

Make Your Own Deep-Dish Pizza

Ingredients

- 3½ cups all-purpose flour
- ¼ cup cornmeal
- ¼ ounce quick-rising yeast
- 1½ teaspoons sugar
- 1 teaspoon salt
- ⅓ cup olive oil
- 3 cups mozzarella cheese
- Parmesan cheese
- 1 28-ounce can of diced tomatoes
- 1 8-ounce can of tomato sauce
- 1 6-ounce can of tomato paste
- Garlic powder
- Dried oregano
- Dried basil
- Pepper

Directions

1. Combine 1½ cups of all-purpose flour, ¼ cup cornmeal, one package (¼ ounce) quick-rising yeast, 1½ teaspoons sugar, and ½ teaspoon salt in a large bowl.
2. Heat 1 cup water and ⅓ cup olive oil in a saucepan. Add the liquid to the dry ingredients and stir briskly until moist. Add another 2 cups of flour.
3. Punch dough down and divide in half. Roll each portion into an 11-inch circle. Press the dough into the bottom and up the sides of two greased 10-inch skillets that can go into the oven. Sprinkle 2 cups of mozzarella cheese over each of the pans of dough.
4. Combine 1 28-ounce can of diced tomatoes, 1 8-ounce can of tomato sauce, and 1 6-ounce can of tomato paste in a large bowl. Add ½ teaspoon salt and ¼ teaspoon each of garlic powder, dried oregano, dried basil, and pepper (adjust seasonings according to your taste). Pour mixture over each of the pans of dough.
5. Add one cup mozzarella cheese to each pie, along with a sprinkling of parmesan cheese.
6. Cover with foil and bake at 450°F for 35 minutes. Then uncover and bake for 5 more minutes.
7. Cut and enjoy!

remained a destination for African Americans for decades.

Today, most African Americans in Illinois do not live in small towns like Brooklyn. More than 97 percent of the state's African Americans live in urban areas. Since the early 1900s, they have formed organizations to promote education and help people find jobs. The Urban League is one example.

African Americans in Illinois have formed other organizations to help children and families make good lives for themselves. In Chicago, Alton, and Bloomington, the organization 100 Black Men coordinates mentoring and other programs for African American children, especially young boys. A mentor is an older or more experienced person who works one-on-one with a younger person and acts as a role model. Members of 100 Black Men groups generally have successful careers. When they meet with students, they talk about things that have helped them set and reach their goals: self-respect, taking responsibility, being part of a healthy community, and education.

Many African American Illinoisans have made significant contributions to the arts. Poet Gwendolyn Brooks was the first African American to win a Pulitzer Prize—a major award for authors, poets, journalists, and composers. Miles Davis (jazz), Mahalia Jackson (gospel), and Muddy Waters (the blues) each helped popularize a different style of music and, in doing so, enriched American culture. Music producer Quincy Jones helped create many famous recordings, including Michael Jackson's *Thriller* album. Popular media figure Oprah Winfrey gained her fame in Chicago. She used her long-running talk show to influence people in many positive ways. Oprah has also used her wealth and power to start charities and to highlight problems in society. With Oprah's Book Club, she has promoted reading and helped sell millions of books.

Diversity in Illinois

Over the past thirty years, many immigrants have moved to Illinois. For example, since the early 1980s, thousands of people from Eastern Europe have come to the state. In fact, Chicago, which has a large Polish-American population, claims to be the world's largest "Polish city" outside Poland.

Large numbers of people from Latin America and Asia have also moved to Illinois in recent decades. Hispanic Americans come to Illinois from many different places: Mexico, Puerto Rico, Venezuela, El Salvador, Colombia, and Guatemala, to name just a few. Asian Americans also come from a wide variety of countries, including India, the Philippines, China, South Korea, Vietnam, and Japan.

Immigrants play an important part in shaping their communities. Some immigrants open stores and restaurants that sell their native foods and goods. One way government and businesses in Illinois help meet the needs of immigrant communities is by promoting businesses run by minorities. Illinois's strength comes from its diversity. It's a state filled with people of all different backgrounds who join together to form strong communities.

Illinois celebrates diversity with events of all kinds. Here, Polish dancers perform at the Constitution Day Parade.

Immigrations and Migrations

Like many states, Illinois's growth was shaped by various waves of immigrants and migrations. The first great wave of European immigrants began arriving in Illinois after 1830. At first, most of the new arrivals were Germans. Many were farmers, drawn by the state's open spaces and fertile farmland. They spread throughout the state, bringing their language and culture with them. By 1850, foreign-born immigrants accounted for 13 percent of the nearly 850,000 people living in Illinois.

The second half of the nineteenth century brought explosive growth. The population of Illinois grew by more than 20 percent each decade. Much of that growth came from immigrants. Germans continued to come in large numbers, joined by Irish and Swedes. By 1860, more than half of Chicago's residents were foreign born.

Illinois's fertile farmland drew thousands of immigrants, especially German immigrants, in the 1800s.

In the second half of the nineteenth century, Africans Americans began migrating from the South to Northern cities. They were drawn by the prospect of better-paying jobs. This migration helped swell the state's population to nearly five million people by 1900.

The early twentieth century brought continued migration of African Americans to Illinois. Meanwhile, immigrants began moving north from Mexico. Many worked on farms. Others flocked to Chicago. In fact, the Chicago metropolitan area now has the fifth-largest number of Spanish-speaking residents among all cities in the country. Meanwhile, increasing numbers of immigrants came from European countries such as Italy and Poland. By 1960, Illinois's total population topped ten million.

Since then, the state's rate of population growth has leveled off. Still, immigrants have continued to arrive. Many of these new immigrants haven come from Eastern Europe, Asia, and Africa. Today, at least 150 languages are spoken in the Chicago metropolitan area, and foreign-born people account for more than 10 percent of Illinois's total population.

Farming is an important industry in Illinois. After farmers grow food, factories around the state process and package it.

4 At Work in Illinois

Illinois is a large state with a large workforce. In fact, the state's civilian workforce totaled nearly 6.7 million people as of August 2018. These people provide a strong talent pool. Workers in Illinois hold many types of jobs, ranging from farming to manufacturing to technology. Meanwhile, jobs in the service industry include a variety of professions ranging from lawyer or teacher to chef or hair stylist. Here are some of the key industries in Illinois.

Agriculture

Agriculture remains a key part of Illinois's economy. Early European American settlers found Illinois to be an excellent place for raising animals and growing crops. An article in an 1843 Illinois newspaper quoted one person who said, "Thousands of hogs was raised without any expense." Another article in the same publication spoke of "the ease with which [corn] is cultivated."

In the pioneer days, most people made their living on small farms. Today, less than 1 percent of Illinoisans work on farms, but the state is still the nation's leading producer of

FAST FACT

In 1837, Illinois blacksmith John Deere developed a new type of plow designed to work in the thick prairie soil of the Midwest. Today, Deere & Company manufactures a wide range of products, including plows, riding mowers, construction vehicles, forestry products, and more. Based in Moline, Deere & Company ranks among the ten largest companies headquartered in Illinois.

The Vienna Beef company makes hot dogs in its Chicago factory.

soybeans, second-largest producer of corn, and fourth-largest producer of hogs. Illinois farmers provide food and food products for people in the United States and around the world.

Unlike the small family-run farms of long ago, today's farms are part of a highly specialized industry. Many farmers hold university degrees and use scientific and technological knowledge to make their farms as productive as possible.

Many Illinoisans who do not work directly on a farm still depend on Illinois agriculture for their jobs. Food-related industries include grain and flour milling, manufacturing food for farm animals and pets, meat processing and packing, and producing processed and packaged foods. These industries are very important to the state's economy. In fact, Chicago is one of the world's leading cities for processing, packaging, and distributing food products.

Manufacturing and Construction

Until the 1980s, thousands of Illinoisans worked in steel mills or factories that manufactured farm, construction, and industrial machinery, transportation equipment, and chemicals. However, over the past few decades, many business owners moved their businesses to other countries, where labor was much cheaper, or closed their factories because their buildings and equipment were old and the cost of replacing them was too high. When manufacturing plants closed in Illinois, many people lost their jobs.

Even so, both manufacturing and construction remain very important industries in Illinois. In addition to food manufacturing industries, Illinois is home to many other manufacturing businesses, which create a wide

Growth and Technology

In 2017, 437,000 people worked in technology-related jobs in Illinois. This means Illinois ranked fifth among all states. Many of the state's top tech companies are centered around the Illinois Technology and Research Corridor. This region stretches across much of the metropolitan area west of Chicago.

But technology jobs aren't the only opportunities in the state. According to *Inc.*, Illinois ranked sixth in the nation in 2017 among states with the largest number of fast-growing companies. That year, Chicago was home to two of the nation's top-ten fastest-growing private companies. One is Home Chef, a home meal delivery service. The other is GForce Life Sciences, which specializes in staffing for pharmaceutical and biotechnology positions.

The Fermi National Accelerator Laboratory in Batavia is part of the Illinois Technology and Research Corridor.

In an attempt to further boost business in the state, Illinois formed a nonprofit called Creating Opportunities for Retention & Expansion (CORE) in 2016. The partnership of businesses, regional economic development groups, and community partners gathers data to help support businesses across the state. In 2016 and 2017, CORE conducted surveys of nearly six hundred businesses across the state. Most were small businesses with fewer than one hundred employees. CORE hopes to use the survey results to help provide support around identified needs. There's no question that Illinois is a great place for tech companies and small businesses.

variety of products. Some companies make heavy machinery. Others make electronics, computers, and computer parts. Others still make objects from cement, concrete, and recycled steel that are used in the construction industry. The state also has paper mills, printers, and publishers. Some companies make medicines, and others make medical instruments. Yet Illinois's biggest manufacturing industry is the chemical industry. Among other products, Illinois chemical manufacturers make fertilizers, ethanol (an automobile fuel), and even chemicals for cleaning polluted water. With all these different kinds of factories, Illinois ranked fifth in the nation in 2018 in number of manufacturing jobs.

The Service Industry and Finance

More than half of Illinois workers are employed in a service industry. Service industries are those whose main business is helping people: hospitals, schools, law firms, insurance agencies, governmental agencies, banks and other financial institutions, hotels, retail stores, and restaurants are a few examples.

Chicago is the financial center of the Midwest. In fact, the US government has a bank there: the Federal Reserve Bank of Chicago. The Chicago Mercantile Exchange and the Chicago Board of Options Exchange play important roles in worldwide investment.

Chicago, along with other cities in Illinois, helps make the state a center for wholesale and retail trade. The state's central location and its strong transportation system help link Illinois to the rest of the country and the world.

Traders make bids at the Chicago Board of Options Exchange.

Sports and Tourism

Illinois's professional sports teams bring a lot of money to the state. Chicago has two famous Major League Baseball teams, the Cubs and the White Sox. The Chicago Blackhawks are one of the original six teams in the National Hockey League. The city's football and basketball teams, the Bears (NFL), the Bulls (NBA) and the Sky (WNBA), have fans all over the country. The Chicago Fire, a Major League Soccer team, also has a loyal following. In addition, fans of auto racing flock to the Chicagoland Speedway in Joliet to watch their favorite racecar drivers.

The Chicago Bears play at Soldier Field.

Tourists come from all over the world to see everything that Illinois has to offer. They may want to see the bustling city of Chicago, the beautiful blue waters of Lake Michigan, or the wilderness in Shawnee National Forest. Tourists and residents alike enjoy kayaking, rock climbing, fishing, and camping in Illinois's many and varied state parks and natural areas. The money that tourists spend in hotels, restaurants, and shops helps boost the economy of the Prairie State.

The University of Chicago is one of the country's top universities.

Education

Education is very important in Illinois— and a big part of the economy. As of 2014, the state had more than five thousand elementary and secondary schools and nearly 2.3 million students in grades pre-K through twelve. Public and nonpublic schools in the state employ about two hundred thousand people.

The University of Illinois has campuses in Chicago, Springfield, and Urbana-Champaign. More than eighty thousand students are enrolled on the three campuses, and thousands more take classes off campus and online. Illinois operates nine other public universities that are scattered throughout the state.

Illinois also has many fine private colleges and universities. The University of Chicago is one of the leading research centers in the country. Some of the top scholars and scientists in the world have taught at or attended the university. President Barack Obama was a professor at the University of Chicago Law School before he was elected to the US Senate. Northwestern University in Evanston is another private university with a top reputation throughout the country. Its graduates include many well-known politicians, business leaders, entertainers, and journalists.

FAST FACT

Headquartered in Chicago, McDonald's is the largest company based in Illinois. To support employees worldwide who want to advance in the company, McDonald's founded Hamburger University in 1961. Since that time, more than eighty thousand people have graduated from this training center.

Energy

Illinois needs a lot of electricity to power its homes and businesses. However, electricity

These wind turbines produce energy in northern Illinois.

production is important in Illinois for another reason. The state makes money by exporting some of the electricity it generates to other states. Today, coal and nuclear power plants provide most of the electricity generated in Illinois. However, burning coal can pollute the atmosphere, and the nuclear power plants in Illinois and across the country are several decades old. They will need to be rebuilt or replaced soon. The state of Illinois is looking at new ways to provide energy.

In recent years, scientists have developed new technologies related to burning coal. Using these technologies, factories and power plants that burn coal can lessen their emissions and help coal-burning power plants become safer and more efficient.

Illinoisans know that it is important to protect the air we breathe, the water we drink, our natural resources, and our wildlife. The state has developed many programs to encourage

Invented in Illinois: The Cell Phone

The next time you pick up your cell phone, you can thank engineer Martin Cooper. A native of Chicago, Cooper is credited with inventing the first mobile cell phone in 1973 while working for Motorola. AT&T had developed cell phone technology, but their phones were attached to cars and could only be used there. Cooper perfected the technology that made cell phones truly portable. He placed the first call to a rival engineer from AT&T.

Martin Cooper invented the cell phone in 1973.

The first mobile cell phone looked far different from today's sleek, multifunction models. The first cell phone could not take pictures. It didn't have apps. It couldn't connect to the internet (the internet wouldn't come into widespread use for another twenty years). Furthermore, the first cell phone wasn't very handy. It stood 9 inches (23 cm) tall and weighed 2.5 pounds (1 kg). Also, you could only talk for about half an hour before the phone needed to be recharged.

A decade later, Motorola introduced the first portable cell phone for consumers. At a cost of nearly $4,000, few people could afford them. Cooper went on to form other companies providing cell phone services and software. In 2013, he received the Draper Prize. This award honors engineering achievements that have improved the quality of life in modern society.

people to protect the environment. Some of these programs encourage the use of renewable energy sources, such as solar and wind power.

Illinois has a program to help people learn about wind energy. The state makes maps that show people how windy it is where they live. They can use the maps to decide whether installing a wind turbine would help them save money on their electricity bill. People who produce more electricity than they use might even be able to make money by selling their extra electricity back to one of Illinois's power companies.

Most schools in Illinois have special environmental awareness programs. Earth Day in the Parks is held at state parks around Illinois each spring. Students at these events may plant trees, restore a local prairie, or even help build a butterfly garden. They enjoy coming back later in the year to see how their project has helped the environment.

Looking to the Future

Like most states, the economy of Illinois improved during the 2010s, following the downturn that began in 2008. However, as of 2018, its unemployment rate still ranked slightly above the national average, and its economy lagged the nation's in terms of growth. Still, the state has a strong agriculture and manufacturing base and continues to invest in technology. Illinois seems poised for a successful future. There will always be buyers for the agricultural and manufactured products that Illinois makes.

The State Capitol in Springfield has been in use since the late 1800s.

5 Government

In many ways, state governments look like the federal (also known as the national) government, except on a smaller scale. The governor leads the state government, just as the president leads the country as a whole. State governments have three parts, or branches: the executive, legislative, and judicial branches. These branches act to balance each other's power, just as at the federal level. The Illinois state government operates out of Springfield, the state capital.

The Executive Branch

The executive branch includes the governor, lieutenant governor, secretary of state, treasurer, comptroller and attorney general. The governor either approves or vetoes (rejects) laws passed by the legislature. The governor and other executive agencies enforce approved laws. The governor also appoints state officials and manages the state budget, which determines where the state spends its money. Governors are elected for four-year terms. Every year, the governor makes a speech called "the State of the State" address. In the speech, the governor talks about Illinois's successes and how to continue them. He

J. B. Pritzker became the governor of Ilinois in 2019.

or she also discusses problems affecting the state and proposes ways to fix them.

The lieutenant governor assists the governor and will take over if the governor cannot complete his or her term. The secretary of state is in charge of all recordkeeping for Illinois, including drivers' licenses and other licenses. The treasurer is in charge of the investment and safekeeping of the state's money. The comptroller keeps financial accounts for the state. The attorney general is the top lawyer for Illinois. He or she helps decide legal matters that are important to the state and its citizens.

The Legislative and Judicial Branches

The Illinois legislature listens to an address by President Barack Obama in 2016.

The Illinois legislature, called the general assembly, makes the state's laws. The general assembly has two houses, both of which must pass a bill before it can become a law. One house, the senate, has 59 members, who are elected to two-year or four-year terms. The other house, called the house of representatives, has 118 members, all of whom are elected to two-year terms.

The judicial branch contains the state's courts. Those courts apply the state's laws in specific cases and decide whether laws agree with the state constitution and are being enforced fairly. The Illinois Supreme Court is the state's highest court. It hears cases that are appealed from lower courts. The state supreme court has seven justices. The circuit courts are the state's lower-level courts. Circuit courts hear cases that involve possible violation of state civil or criminal laws. Circuit court decisions can be appealed to a state appellate court. In Illinois, the main judges are elected for all the state's courts. However, judges in the circuit court can appoint associate judges to help them hear cases. Illinois's supreme and appellate court judges are elected for ten-year terms. Circuit court judges are elected for six-year terms. Associate judge appointments are four-year terms.

Courts, like this one, are part of the judicial branch of government.

From Bill to Law

State legislators propose laws (called bills until they are passed) to address state issues. Sometimes the ideas behind a bill come from the state's residents. If a person or a group of people think that a new law needs to be passed, they might circulate a petition. A petition is a formal written request that is signed by people who want the request carried out. The petition describes how the signers would like the state to deal with their issue. It may suggest wording for a new law. When the petition has hundreds of signatures, the people circulating the petition send it to their representatives in the Illinois house and senate.

The legislators in Springfield gauge public interest in the issue. If they receive a lot of phone calls, emails, letters, or petitions about it from the people they represent, they might work with their staff and other legislators to draft, or write, a bill. A bill is a proposal for a new law.

Citizens can sign petitions asking the state to address issues of concern.

A bill may be introduced in the senate or the house. A bill needs to be read three times in both the senate and the house. First, the bill is introduced and read. The second time it is read is a chance to make amendments, or changes. The third reading comes right before a vote.

The bill has to pass by a simple majority each time it comes up in both bodies of the legislature.

Even when both the senate and the house pass a bill, the versions that the two houses pass may not be exactly the same. In this case, senators and representatives form a committee to combine the two versions into one final bill. The new bill must again pass in both bodies of the legislature.

Bruce Rauner served as governor from 2015 to 2019. Here, Governor Rauner signs a bill into law.

Once a bill is passed in the senate and the house, it is sent to the governor within thirty days. He or she has sixty days to sign the bill into law or veto it. The governor can also choose to do nothing, but then the bill becomes a law after the sixty days have passed. After a veto, there's still a chance the bill will become a law. The general assembly needs to vote to override a veto. It requires three-fifths of senators and representatives in each chamber to vote "yes" to override the governor's veto.

Congress

Like all other states, Illinois voters choose people to represent them in the US Congress in Washington, DC. Illinois voters elect two US senators who serve six-year terms. In 2018, Illinois had eighteen representatives in the US House of Representatives. Representatives serve two-year terms. A state's population determines its number of representatives.

As of 2019, Illinois has two senators and eighteen representatives in Congress.

Using Technology to Get Involved

The internet makes it easier than ever before to learn what's happening in state government and keep in touch with your state representatives and senators. Listings and links on the Illinois.gov website make contacting elected officials by email a snap. The site also provides links to all bills being considered during each session of the legislature. Additionally, you can find listings and contact information for members of all legislative committees.

Want to keep up with the governor? Follow him on Facebook, Twitter, and Instagram. (Remember to ask a trusted adult before logging on to social media.) As of 2018, the governor had more than fifty thousand Facebook likes and more than thirty thousand Twitter followers. People can also sign up to get regular email updates from the governor.

Your elected officials want to hear from you, even if you're too young to vote. Many ideas for important new laws come from young people. If you are concerned about an issue facing Illinoisans, do research. Find out how lawmakers are addressing your concern. If you have an opinion about what lawmakers should do differently, reach out. Democracies count on people getting involved.

Illinois.gov lists all the bills from a general assembly session.

Key Issues for the Future

As in many states, financial issues rank among the key concerns for Illinois legislators. Illinois faces some challenges. In 2017, Illinois ranked forty-ninth among all states in terms of overall financial condition. It had a budget deficit of $14.6 billion. Simply put, the state was spending more money than it was taking in through taxes and other revenues.

In 2018, Illinois tried to pass a balanced budget for 2019, where income and expenses were equal. However, the state ended up passing a budget that was likely to spend $1.2 billion more than Illinois would earn that year. To help create a balanced budget for future years, the state increased tax rates for both individuals and corporations beginning in 2018. Some people are concerned that higher income taxes, along with already-high property tax rates, may discourage people and businesses from being in Illinois. Others say the taxes are an important step toward balancing the budget.

Glossary

artifact An object made by a human being that is of cultural or historical interest.

assassinated Killed for political reasons.

Cahokia The city where a great civilization of Mississippian people thrived long before European settlers came to America.

Chicagoland An informal name used to describe the city of Chicago and its surrounding suburbs. The term sometimes includes eight nearby Illinois counties as well as parts of Indiana and Wisconsin.

ethanol A grain alcohol that can be blended with gasoline and used in motor vehicles. Most of the ethanol made in the United States comes from corn grown in the Midwest.

Great Depression A period of severe worldwide economic decline that took place in the decade (1930s) just before World War II.

immigrants People who leave one country and come to another to live there.

mounds Earth piled up into rounded hills on which Cahokians constructed temples, government buildings, and homes of their leaders.

nomadic Anything that moves around a lot, usually referring to hunter-gatherer tribes that follow the animals they hunt.

nuclear Relating to the nucleus of an atom, or to something powered by nuclear energy. Nuclear energy is used to generate heat for producing steam. The steam turns a turbine that generates electricity.

reservation An area of land marked for use by Native Americans.

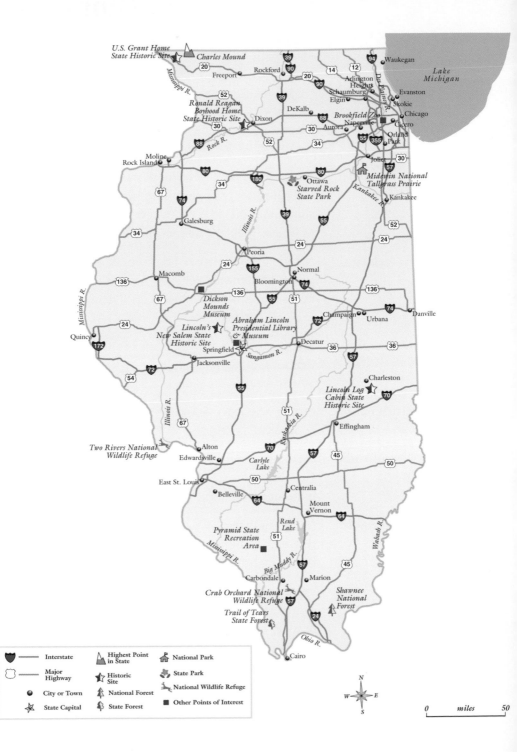

Map Skills Questions

1. What is the highest point in Illinois?

2. What is the southernmost city or town?

3. Which direction is Champaign from Urbana?

4. What is the westernmost city or town?

5. Chicago is on the banks of what body of water?

6. What highway would you take to get from Macomb to Rock Island?

7. Charles Mound is east of what point of interest?

8. Which city or town is south of Normal?

9. What point of interest is north of Effingham?

10. What interstate would you take to get from Belleville to East St. Louis?

Answers:

1. Charles Mound
2. Cairo
3. West
4. Quincy
5. Lake Michigan
6. Highway 67
7. U.S. Grant Home State Historic Site
8. Bloomington
9. Lincoln Log Cabin State Historic Site
10. Interstate 64

More Information

Books

Kortemeier, Todd. *It's Great to Be a Fan in Illinois*. Sports Nation. Mendota Heights, MN: North Star Editions, 2018.

Otfinoski, Steven. *The Great Chicago Fire: All Is Not Lost*. Tangled History. North Mankato, MN: Capstone, 2018.

Santella, Andrew. *Illinois Native Peoples*. Portsmouth, NH: Heinemann, 2007.

Skipworth, Mark, and Lloyd, Christopher. *The Illinois Chronicles*. Kent, UK: What on Earth Books, 2018.

Websites

Illinois Attorney General Kids' Page
http://www.illinoisattorneygeneral.gov/children/kids/index.html
Find trivia, information about Illinois's government, and links to official Illinois websites on this page hosted by the state's attorney general.

Illinois State Museum
http://www.illinoisstatemuseum.org
Browse online collections, find information about visiting the museum, and more on this site.

Official Illinois State Tourism Website
http://www.enjoyillinois.com
Learn about special events in the state and exciting attractions.

Index

Page numbers in **boldface** refer to images. Entries in **boldface** are glossary terms.

Addams, Jane, 38, **38**
African Americans, 6–7, 32, 38, 45, 52, 54–55, 57
agriculture, 9–10, **10**, 12–13, 16–18, 20–21, **21**, 24, 30, 32, 35, 37, 40, 42–43, 45–46, **46**, 56–57, **56**, **58**, 59–60, 67
American Revolution, 29–30
architecture, 5, 15, 35, 47
artifact, 15
Asian Americans, 42, 55, 57
assassinated, 39
Aurora, 12, **12**

Black Hawk, 31, **31**, 34, 38
Brooklyn, 52, 54
Brooks, Gwendolyn, 38, **38**, 54
budget, 69, 74

Cahokia, **22**, 24–25, **25**, 28–29
Cairo, 11, **11**
canals, 34–35
cell phones, 66, **66**
Chicago, 4–7, **8**, 9, 11–15, **15**, 17, 34–35, **34**, **35**, 37–41, **37**, **42**, 43, **44**, 46–48, **47**, **48**, 50–51, 54–57, 60–63, **60**, **62**, 64, **64**, 66
Chicago International Film Festival, 41, **41**
Chicagoland, 12, 46
Civil War, 5, 32–34, **32**, 39
Clark, George Rogers, 29–30, **30**
climate, 14, 16
construction, 60, 62
Cooper, Martin, 66, **66**

Davis, Miles, 38, 54
Deere, John, 35, 59
department stores, 37, **37**
Douglas, Stephen A., 33, **33**

education, 41–42, 47–48, **47**, 50–51, 54, 62, 64, 67
electricity, 12, 40, 64–65, **65**, 67
endangered species, 18–19, **19**
erosion, 16
ethanol, 20, 62

Fermi, Enrico, 39–40, **40**
finance, 62, 70, 74
fishing, 10–11, 14, 63
flooding, 14, 16, **16**
food processing, 37, 60, **60**
forests, 9–10, 16, 18–19, 28, 63
French and Indian War, 28–29, **29**
French colonists, 4, 13, 17, 25–26, 28–30

Galena, 12, 46, **46**
gangsters, 40
German Americans, 56
glaciers, 10
government
    federal, 7, 17, 23, 27, 31–34, 39, 43, 46, 62, 64, 69, 72
    state, 6, 13, 55, **68**, 69–74, **70**, **71**, **72**
Grant, Ulysses S., 5, 23, 33
Great Chicago Fire, 4, 35
Great Depression, 37, 40

Hispanic Americans, 42, 45, 55, 57

Illinois Technology and Research Corridor, 61
immigrants, 12, 38, 42, 55–57

industrialization, 35, 37

Jolliet, Louis, 4, 17, **17**, 25, 28

Lincoln, Abraham, 5–6, 13, 23,
    31, 33–34, **33**, **34**, 39

Magnificent Mile, 15, **15**
manufacturing, 12, 32, 35, 37,
    39–40, 59–60, 62, 67
Marquette, Jacques, 4, 17, **17**, 25, 28
McCormick, Cyrus, 35, 39, **39**
Michigan, Lake, 9, 11–15, 17,
    25–26, **26**, 28, 63
Mississippian culture, 24–25, **25**
Mormons, 49, **49**
mounds, **22**, 24
museums, 6, 15, **15**, 46
music, 5, 27, 38, 43, 54

Native Americans, 23–28, **25**, **26**,
    29, 31, **31**, 34, 38, 49, 52
Nauvoo, 49, **49**
nomadic, 23–24
Northwest Territory, 17, 30
nuclear, 5, 39–40, 65

Obama, Barack, 7, 23, 64, **70**
Obama, Michelle, 51, **51**
100 Black Men, 54
Ozarks, 10

plant life, 5, **5**, 16–17, 19–20, **20**, 24, 67
Polish Americans, 55, **55**
population, 4, 12–13, 31, 45, 49, 54–57
poverty, 38, 40, 42, 47

railroads, 34–35
religion, 28, 49
renewable energy, 65, **67**
reservation, 31
rivers
    Illinois, 10–11, **14**, 28

    Mississippi, 9–11, 14, 16–17,
        17, 24, 28–30, 34, 37
    Ohio, 9, 11, **11**, 17, 30
    Wabash, 9, 11, 17

service industry, 59, 61–62
settlement houses, 38
Shawnee National Forest,
    10–11, **11**, 63
skyscrapers, 5, 35
slavery, 32–34, 52
sports, 6–7, 10, 27, 43, 51, 63, **63**
Springfield, 4, 6, 13, 33–34, **34**,
    43, 64, **68**, 69, **70**, 71
statehood, 4, 7, 17, 23, 31, 42–43
stockyards, **35**, 37, 60
suburbs, 12, 40, 42, 45–47
Swedish Americans, 12, 56

technology, 59–61, 65–67, 73
tornadoes, 16
tourism, 12–13, 15, 19, 49, 60, 63

unemployment, 37, 40, 47, 67
universities, 5, 13, 40, 46–48,
    48, 50, 52, 64, **64**

wildlife, **6**, 7, 14, 18–19, **18**,
    19, 21, **21**, 27, 65
women's rights, 5, 37, 39
World War I, 37
World War II, 37, 40